LEGION OF LOST LETTERS

# LEGION
# OF LOST LETTERS

## DRAMATIC MONOLOGUES
## OF ROMANS IN EXILE

# DEBASISH LAHIRI

THE **BLACK SPRING**
PRESS GROUP

First published in 2023
by The Black Spring Press Group
Eyewear Publishing imprint
Maida Vale, London W9,
United Kingdom

*Typeset and graphic design by* Edwin Smet

978-1-915406-42-2

BLACKSPRINGPRESSGROUP.COM

TO MY FATHER
WHO TAUGHT ME HOW UNCOMMONLY BEAUTIFUL
THE ORDINARY CAN BE.

# TABLE OF CONTENTS

# INTRODUCTION

Can we imagine the surly Roman legionnaire, manning a coign on Hadrian's Wall, immune to the moods of the air, but sunk, abysmally, in his own visions? — Part of a stately iconography and devoid of their human frailties, these men from Rome, and many other women and men besides, who were shipped north in the service of the empire, to Britain, led unremarkable lives, while the brimstone of their loves, hates, fears, desires and losses never quite kindled or exploded at their passing. *Legion of Lost Letters* is a journey, both backwards and forwards, an attempt to reinvigorate this silence until it buzzes into life, an attempt to revivify a way of life.

If contemplation were a conduit and one could walk through it long enough, time travel would become a possibility. In *Legion of Lost Letters*, ordinary lives and the extraordinary weight of their disaffections, frustrations, regrets and hopes, largely in situations from Roman Britain, are burnished into legend by an act of imagination.

Moving through the puckered stone of Roman ruins in the present, the poet unearths rumpled vestments of the human heart buried there, making the ruins revenant. On the leeward side of heraldry and historical oversight, women and men, lovers and misanthropes, unwilling gladiators and unlikely saints, doomed dreamers and gullible aesthetes thrive in the pages of *Legion of Lost Letters*. These forgotten beings from beyond the millennial horizon ponder the second millennium. The light of these lives, effigies of breathing, made pale and frail by time, resonate in *Legion of Lost Letters*: a light that is not yet loud enough to be heard.

DEBASISH LAHIRI
October 2022

## OVID CONTEMPLATES WRITING
## HIS FASTI AT TOMIS

My poets visit me like the night,
every day. They obtrude
when I can grip my iron quill
and syllables grow warm on my tongue
like my fingers in rare fire-lit hours.
They seem to know,
better than Caesar's spies,
when Nasso breathes and sighs,
when he is reminded of verse
by his own still-warm blood
and its pulse inside his scarecrow bosom.
Perhaps, they are of Caesar too,
or do I have snow-drift in my imagination?

They will appear during the sunless hours
of the day,
they will accost me like that legion
of minutes that jostle at dawn's mouth
expecting the sun,
or at my cell door, singing in the wind's borrowed voice,
prophecy the rage of frost and flint
on Roman shin and skin.

They used to whisper love's caprices in my ears,
louder than the din near the Capitol.
They proclaimed the wisdom of love,
silent,
like the fall of eastern silk
and myrrh-laughter
in alcoves and breathless covertures
in great palaces. —

Here, no shuttle of nectarine branches on a summer loom
weaves a curtain round love's bower,
keeping Caesar from the greater voyeur,
the sun. – No trees grow here
to give Nasso a sense of perspective.
The far and the near are far enough
for my reach.
My memories of Rome not near enough
for verse.

Time in Tomis is blizzard or the convict wind,
escaped from the warden of every quadrant.
In my anguish, cold eyes closed
and a grimace curling my lips
like the slow, deliberate swell of the fog,
I am a reed of memory:
my every breath a semi-tone of time. –

The gutted taper remains my only witness.

I do not need light,
only my fingers.

And then like the burning eyes
and salt-snow, I suddenly lose everything,
love, memory, Rome, Tomis, everything,
except Caesar and my poets
who will make me talk when I crave quiet
and empty me of words
when my lyre-shaped heart is a-twang with babble
like a cup of libation drained before a thirsty god.

My poets gag me when I read casual quotations
recorded in earlier encomium-days.
My attempt at lament forgets this tryst with languor,

this languor in ice.
Instead I find a garden of burnt September grass
and dark, hot shades,
jets of laughter and the murmur of brawling love
reciting its rites between the crush of leaves.

Caesar, the poet's gold,
is the pestilent dew in my ribs.
My spittoon glows in the dark. —

My poets know that,
and from the soft spines of old books
they stall my verse
like the promise of early spring
that makes jealous winter furrow the land
in angry gloom.

I have written this journal of the interim,
the interim of the day-to-day.
Let Caesar and his poets have their day,
let me write the interim.

(Tomis, c. 7 A.D.)

## SYCAMORE GAP

The mountains are armed today with wind.
They change weapons from hand to hand,
left, right, left. They stand on
one leg, or two. They play games
with the snow but, being like Laberius,
our commander, a Minotaur, a very Antaeus,
I do not think the mountains
play at hide and seek.
Aella did.
When she first came through the gap
in the wall
hiding behind the black heather
of her hair,
I feared that she was one
of the faceless women I had heard of
in stories at the camp;
Palinurus's arch-brow'd stories,
burning like cressets in a dark porch,
burning his eyes and ours,
stories about the spirits
of faceless women among the Celts.
And then the wind blew
from the left, West that is,
where the sun occasionally sets.
Often he lets a cloud cover his retreat
and like a true Roman
his feet go truly home
though away from home.
The wind blew
and I was relieved
that Aella had a face, though a Celt's.
She was smiling

and peeping
from behind the bracken-bearded rocks.
Her approach was hidden
and she sought me.
She was playing, even then.
Only it took me all these years
to realize.
I was barely out of my teens.
My helmet held my head
like a roasted nut,
too small for its shell.
My Adam's apple was a pain
in my throat at the end
of long sentences.
My knees were like stones in a river bed,
round and angular,
without the promise of grace.

★

For many years, the gap in the hill,
that mossy cleft in our emperor's
bold wall, let Aella in,
and me, out of my turret,
outside the scope of that mile-castle,
that Varro, the surly cynic of these walls
manned. Aella was a child,
but stood like a pile of snow
on the firm rock, soft, yet poised.
She beckoned to me,
ungainly Roman, to chase her
through the gap and into the Celt's turf.
I often did. I tremble
in fear now that I remember.
But the grass then seemed

to have a tang of sweat;
sweat was grass and the cold air
a panting relief after the chase:
pursuer and quarry laughing
the emperor's tall wall down,
rocking the turrets and forts
of Britannia like a tub
of hot soup that Piraeus
can never set down without
tilting.

     ★

The years have passed like the clouds
waving mischief over the moon's face,
slowly:
so slowly, that I often lay breathless
trying to bring my breathing down
to their pace.
The moon shone on these rare summer nights.
The hills threw down their
armaments of wind. I was in the turret,
amazed by this eastern moon;
looking up at this wild light
that threatened me, looking down
upon the sleepless barbarity of the Celt
as Flaccus growled and whistled
through his nose, making loneliness
lonelier.

     ★

Aella's father was the barbarian chief.
His tall black beard and huge
hairy arms frightened me: shameful

though it is for a Roman. No less
than fifteen of our squadron
he had killed singly. The
heavy axe he carried seemed
crushing like the weight of these mountains,
cold like the coming of autumn after summer.
I have been offered promotions
before. – I was asked to accept
the position of captain in our legion,
the offer being a chance to move
to Gaul, where the fighting was worse,
but a sure path to Rome, not too late.
I refused. I was not worthy,
I suggested. Really, I thought
it was not worth leaving,
leaving Aella and myself behind,
even to Rome. For what would I
do in Rome? My father, Flammius,
burnt the fingers of Rome,
and then himself,
stealing the tithes of three provinces,
and then to celebrate this thing well done,
he went to a band of gypsies
to learn how to mouth fire.
With wine flowing down his gums
like water down frowning rocks,
here, in spring, he bit into fire. –
It set his mouth and face ablaze.
The flaming thief of Rome was a sight
Romans beheld with wonder,
wonder that held its breath,
letting this hectic, shouting candle
burn itself to a gutter.
Well, my mother adorned this soot
of melancholy and from another gutter

of another taper brought me forth.
Helvia longed for that fire
ever since, but had to be content
with my ashen face.
There was nothing in Rome
that called me by name.
But Aella
knew my name,
had taught herself to pronounce
a Roman noun perfectly.
My pallour did not disappoint her.
She warmed with a fire
of her own that sufficed
for both of us. Who says
that Rome is South and warm?
This wall is the Sun's promenade
and our gap is a hill
mellowed by olives.

＊

Varro has made me famous. –
'The Roman legionnaire who plays
hide and seek with a barbarian wench',
'A boy who has grown grizzled hair',
'A barbarian's paramour', 'The Celt's toy' –
many a name, and many
a guffaw that greeted it
kept the spirits high
in mile-castle and turret
when drink and fires were low
and winter in full-throated ease.
I am happy that my humble name
has thawed the seasons, turned
their tide, and brought summer

in their hearts despite the rant
of the cold breeze.
My name has been a zephyr
let loose by Varro, at my expense.
I am happy.

★

But then ten and five years
of this myth's vanity
was at an end. That afternoon
I found Aella again,
as a woman. We were playing.
Wild, animal sounds of joy
leavened with Latin
made the cold air bewildered
as it ducked and weaved
round our caprice. Aella's rough
coat of stiff fur had loosened
round her hips. It was
too short anyway. Hacked
without skill from some animal:
barely protecting,
merely an excuse for a dress.
Aella had refused any gifts
before. She was at her
most rueful then. Her small
ivory hips, mud splattered
and blue with cold still
undulated proudly with the fury
of our play. Our games were
our strange, grammarless language.
The rest was grunts and nods and smiles.
But I swear,
I understood her better than

Laberius's tired speeches.
He seemed to use Latin
as one uses a horse, but in a dream:
imagining great speed
straddling his bed.
I held Aella
that afternoon. The Sun had left
early, like Vaccus, our captain,
early for his gambling. But it was
twilight. The hour they say
anything can happen. In this
gap in time, we stood
at the mouth of the gap
under a sycamore tree.
There was twilight in Aella's eyes.
My fingers found a little island
of hair, like a narrow thicket of mane
on her back. Just where you wear
your belt. Every time I rushed
my fingertips through it she laughed,
and then she leapt away. I chased.
It was destined. It was our play.
But she was too fleet
and the twilight darkened into evening.

       *

Next morning Flaccus was a bell
in my ear. He would not say much
but hauled me to the turret
and said, 'See'. Although he never
cried, as I did, I must say
he was sincere. He did not laugh. –
There was Aella, on a rock,
knees bent as in worship,

her head crushed by a stone,
her neck half-wedged in her shoulders;
and there the barbarian father beside:
god and executioner. Killing to save
the honour of his brood: this girl
who had defiled it by loving a Roman boy.

★

I, Quintus Flammius, wait at this gap.
My legion has left for Gaul.
More killing to do. I am not good at that.
I have stood guard too long. I am a watcher.
I watch over whatever is left
after Time's banquet:
odds and ends of things,
rags, memories, stones,
sweat, grass, squirrel's hair on Aella's back
and sycamore tree. I did not know
that it could be witness to so much sadness.

(Hadrian's Wall, Northumberland, c. 107 A.D.)

## AT DEVA

The tale of summer had been minor skirmishes with the sun.
The spring had been a tale of minor skirmishes
with the Barbarians.
Summer trapped large fish in shallow pools.
The soldiers forded the river
and bore back an unspeakable load,
thrashing like the fish,
to our now autumn-long waiting
called Deva, Deva fort,
a broken neck of rock
piled on with more rocks and fear.
Here we waited for the emperor
and his elephants.

When the first ship slid silently
out of the mist
the guard choked on his warning cry.
Gasping and spitting
he gestured the galleys uncertainly ashore.
Behind loomed creatures that looked
magnified in the lens of mist,
dark and ponderous of gait,
alien behemoths that roused the garrison
with their shrill cries.
Other ships and the emperor followed.
Twelve in all,
these elephants snorted and sucked
at the mists of Albion
and having grown suddenly truculent
tried to board the galley again.
They had a good mind to return
where they came from, perhaps.
Already they had fallen foul of the land.

On that first ship were two lofty elephants
and a slender stalk of a young man,
crouching,
not Roman,
but dark, long haired and tall
when he stood erect,
which was not often.

The soldiers on board greeted the elephants
with cries of, 'Off Pavanus',★
and, 'Go Maurutus',★★
but the beasts would not budge.
Eventually, the dark one
whispered in some strange tongue
and the elephants distended with joy.
They raised their trunks,
swayed their heads,
and flapped their ears,
trampled a cur to death
and had that guard's guts splattered
all over the garrison wall.

They were in Deva's fold.
Pavanus weaved tapestries in the air with his trunk
that terrified the general Gaius Commodus,
who all but lost his footing,
and certainly his grace,
trying to run through the silt,
Claudius an amused spectator.
'As proud as Pavo the peacock,
no bent knees even in my presence',
joked Claudius with his generals.
Maurutus, meanwhile, ground his feet
on the corner of the guard house

and pelted the soldiers with a storm of damp earth.
'Must have been named after that soldier in Egypt,
a disgrace to Rome, surely', the Optio, bald and bony-faced
hissed out. –
'Went by the name of Maurus didn't he,
the one that became a Christian
and would not speak fair of the Roman deities
even when he was faced with death?' –
the forked whisper was loud as an outcry. –
'They pared him down, member by member
till, they say, his severed head adored the Christ
like Orpheus's singing head.' –
'And that grim boy', the Centurion pointed,
'looks like all the winters have left
their debris in him:
him we call Canadus'.
'Ah! Born of the Ethiopian Queen, no doubt',
the pedant Optio was pleased with his wit. –
'Let us amaze these barbarians into submission',
Claudius's voice rang like the north-wind through camp.
'What a circus', grumbled a soldier
up in the turret
and adjusted his furs to the dusk's summon.

The fires burnt high,
fed with the fat of the camp bestiary.
Dinner was a warm glow
that the barbarians felt in frosted dreams
hard by.
And Canadus had gone mad.
'Deva! Deva, Deva, Deva, Deva?',
he wanted to memorise it
or lose all by repeating.
Any Roman hard of hearing would have been cured.
'Come Canadus, this is Deva.

It is our fortress,
not a person you seem to know',
the laughing and the sympathetic held him down.
Canadus, like a damp log
that spits and flares and then hides its fire
in bark and indifferent wood,
hunched moodily by the fire.
It seemed a pair of eyes
glazed by the salt of far oceans
had caught fire
and burnt blue-green
on the cold courtyard of the sky
where memory lamented that it remembered so little.
All its words had broken in silence.

Canadus was not always known by that name.
His birth was indeed a far cry from Africa.
No Ethiopian Queen brought him into the world.
His mother had a five-petalled flower blooming
between her brows,
and her hair smelt of the anemone
that grew by the river.
She was called Swati.
Her son had the smile of a sage,
the frown of a god
and played with elephants on the river.
He was called Kanad.
That was twelve years ago.
He was a boy, then.

Pawan and Marut were the king's elephants,
born in the royal stables
to whom Kanad sang the songs he had learnt
from his mother. –
And when those two elephants were sent to the mighty Parthian

across the salt mere,
Kanad, oblivious of his destiny,
hid in the ship's commodious gut
thinking this to be some innocent prank
whose resolution would see his father
fetching the dusty, balled up knot of man and beast
that were the three kindred spirits,
back to the hot afternoon yard of his mother's stories.

The moody fit never quite dispelled.
The sea was too violent in its green calm,
too brown in its unrelenting vastness.
That journey has reached our fortress today,
to Albion, led by the emperor.

Many languages like the knots in Kanad's hair
that can scarce be untangled,
only shaved away,
hold Kanad steadily on history's rocking boat,
sliding, barely holding on.

Quite unbeknown to himself
Kanad has proved the wise man's words
whose name he bears.
Canadus, strewn across salt and sand,
of time and geography, compass and cutlass,
is his last, indivisible self tonight:
Kanad – Canadus – Nobody,
Roman – Parthian – Indian,
an impossible survival, like a story
that thrives in a crevice of history.

Deva was Canadus's god,
who lived, a cool green shadow of the underground chamber,
where large white flowers and yellow smoke hid his dark body

in faraway temples of his boyhood
where his mother held his fingers
and counted them like beads.

It was late-evening.
'Lay off that mad rant, boy',
Quintus the Bull called out,
bull-necked, a great gutter for the stale vats.
'Deva is our Roman name for this odd angle of land,
not your lost god found again,
swept up by the dolphins from the East.' –
Quintus glowed like fireflies on the river bank
at this rare phlegm of poetry
that had suddenly risen up in his throat.

My indivisible man,
the much-buffeted, much-scattered
and as-much-gathered-up Canadus
had spilled his time like a shattered hourglass that bleeds its sand,
silently,
muffled like the dew from the glare of emperor, general and clown
on a night the camp poets proclaimed
that the heavens were blue and bare
because the celestium of Roman chivalry was all on earth.

Canadus, blue and bare again that night,
proclaimed nothing,
and waited for nothing
like poetry should.

I am an old gossip in Deva fortress.
Onward two score years have I now weathered
the tides of this river.
The emperor that was is dead
and a new emperor commands the soldiery

across half the world.
The elephants came and conquered.
Some were slaughtered by the barbarians,
for an ignoble barbecue most likely.
Canadus and his elephants I never saw again:
divided by realms, sea-passages and river-crossings,
desert-trudges, royal caprices and caparisons of quiet,
the only indivisible man I have known. –

My only claim to wisdom.

(Deva/Chester, c. 66 A.D.)


* Pavana was the Hindu God of the Wind.
** Maruta was a Hindu deity of high winds.

# THE EPISTLE OF MARTINAUS HOSTILIUS

### I

I want to be the person I am today.
I have just written a very long letter.
I must be very sick.
I am of the sick whom one can count on
and believe when I say
that I have written in one afternoon
about the duration of death
that I have spent a life in lengthening.

### II

It was afternoon when this ragged shirt of skin,
that had once been a soldier
was slit through by a Silures sword.
Late that evening,
with the snow on the ground
all rust-smelling
and soft with my blood,
and the fire a cold, yellow fever
on my lidless eyes,
our surgeon, Gaius Picus,
pecked at my torn left arm
and sewed it back
swearing that the legend of Osiris
would have been different
had he been around.

### III

Somewhere in the gloam of my burst pod of flesh
my Roman courage had spilled out.
It must be staining
some cornice of Y 'Gaer,

darker than the stone,
lighter than the day
that feels like a tombstone
at the sun's burial.

IV

And ever since
the right arm shakes
and snatches
like I was attempting to write
in a nightmare.
And so I have written this afternoon
when I can feel change
as a torpor whose past
I cannot imagine,
whose future I cannot see
over this dark green valley
of Usk.

V

I wrote to my wife
in her orange-scented villa
where the walls are white
and the breeze warm
even in winter
because I hear my daughter
singing to her doll
an Euboean song
her mother sang to me
when I was home
and bathed, and smelt
of holly and not of barbarian guts,
ate olives and played
Hercules and Atlas with my cousins
in a garden where I had

grown taller than the bushes
of columbine.

VI

I wrote to my wife:
I asked her if her sibylline song
had any stanza
about blue lips and white knuckles,
unyielding scabbards
and crimson icicles of blood
in our fort of fear,
in this dear, alien Cymru.

VII

I have written to my wife:
'Who am I for you after so many years?' –
'A phantom', I wrote
and added twelve blank sheets
before I signed my name:
enough space for the bald snow,
the bare un-uddered earth
here,
not motherly like the Tiber fields
beside a strict Rome.
Phantoms are made as well here
as in Rome,
thus.

VIII

Martinaus Hostilius,
I want to walk after you
when you are dead,
ex epistulae;
turn around and trace
the turn of the road

from Sarn Helen to the Capitol,
trace the vines and the moss in the Underworld
of the Sun's tenure.

(The Usk Valley, December c. 73 A.D.)

## AT CAERLEON: CAMP

Slabs of slate over a pair of blue eyes:
the sky was closed like an open grave,
white dirt and green grass
and the memory of sleeping together
at Llanmelin Wood possessed it utterly.

★

Shopkeepers,
in this hollow cairn in Rome's ribcage,
smiled at my slow wonder,
smiled at a tourist
reeling from relics:
shopkeepers,
who'd been here since the prodigal comets left,
been here at their homecoming,
at home in Caerleon and Newport –
home nowhere.

★

Daybreak was a thinning of the blood
in the marrow of the East.
Isca Fluvius wiped her sleeve
across our faces.
Our sleep fell athwart the return
of the tide.
'Be the water', our sages gurgled
to us, the people of the stone.
The Romans call us Silures:
they fear the fire-flies in our swords
and the white scree in our eyes.

Our eyes and swords now swell
the Roman menagerie.
The bold Silures of the Ash-shade
and the Apple-bark
perform our lives for peeping Romans
at Caerwent.

Julius Frontinus, impresario, soldier,
sells camp life to his guests:
tired of their purple-clad theatre they ride around camp
to see us in our hovels,
the amphitheater of Roman bondage,
so roomy that it is always at your throat.

I, Caradog, last of the Silures youth,
(the last daughter of the Silures, Angharad,
dying suddenly like the autumn glow
among the hazel last evening,
pink like flesh, red like its kindling),
make this supplication to the closed lids
of the sky. –

The Silures have passed. The river has witnessed it.
The oak-hill and the elm-glen shall be gnarled with our sinews.
The broken moon over the Usk
shall be the broken escarpment of our tired shoulders.
The Silures have passed. Dead like a daffodil
in a Roman urn, –
daffodils that lift
the cowl of mountain mist away
and sing warm songs to a freezing land,
untimely;
daffodils in rootless Roman urns
tended by vinegar fingers

in old, bluff, red-veined afternoon light
that records decay at speechless Roman windows.
The Silures have passed.
So may the Romans.

★

Like a gong on the High Street
the shopkeeper's laugh sent waves up the Usk,
like no sea does.
The shopkeeper saw unfold,
a tale untold
of Mrs. Williams,
yarn spun with the glue,
of vintage seventeen seventy-two.

Mrs. Williams who swung on the tide,
a flood
when the river broke down in tears,
but she survived,
cut through the fabric of foam
with fingers for shears.

How was Mrs. Williams saved?
I had to ask.

She was looking for her mooning husband,
up-town, when she felt towed –
towed, dragged, snatched by the tide
that was till then knocking on doors,
uncertainly,
in mid-town.
Her lantern and voice made awful music
till they fished her out
before she sang

in the Bristol Channel
like Orpheus dissolved,
a sea swilled between her flesh and skin.

Would that not be a going home?
All rivers end in the sea,
don't they? –
Not all rivers.
Some only seek the sea.

A reminder,
from a shopkeeper
that Mrs. Williams lived,
but not the Silures,
on a cold High Street
in Caerleon.

(Caerleon, c. 77 A.D.)

# A PRAYER FOR NEMESIS

A work-a-day sun shone on me
every night.
The sunlight as a butterfly,
the moth as a star
entered my room's seasons.
I am Marcus Aelius,
born on a Roman road,
bred on a Roman villa
and killed in a Roman amphitheatre.
This is my prayer,
also my curse:
this is my story that will condemn you
to memory.

My life was sheltered from the cold
by the burning letters:
I was lost in the summer, spring and autumn
of books.
That strange leafy palm of land,
that last cold tether of lichen and mold
before the white crags
and the white wind
that wipes clean the distinctions
of Barbarian and Roman,
was my home.
It was not Rome though,
as my cousin Caius Hortensius
proclaimed on the villa steps,
where I taught him rules of change,
the calculus of Eudoxus,
before the unchanging vespers.

On rare summer evenings
when the sun grew dark
in his own blood-light
and desperately raged against sleep,
I walked out of the villa
and listened to the natives,
tumbling in their country consonants.

On cold autumn mornings
when icicles were blue
around every surviving stalk
and my fingers,
I wondered through the window
about the lavender fields I knew well,
yet did not know.

All this returns to me
as I stand in this pit
before you, Nemesis,
goddess of the pit and the spire,
sand on my hands,
a dull, dry palate
and a small grey heart-puddle
of mud and fear
somewhere in my body.

Hortensius died longing for the sun,
who was away too long.
And I, Aelius, without my garden
raged like snow in August:
the sweat of a rock.

The villa sighed like silver birches
under a silver moon.

and what was grief's quiet note
the wolves picked up in uproar.

I, Marcus Aelius, was sent west
and north
like all other villa things,
bust and statue.

The north-west required legionnaires.
I was an idler.
I carried buckles, armour and helmets,
for I was too wee to wear them.
I carried swords and javelins,
for I never knew how to wield them.
I boiled hot water
for the surgeons,
murmuring my Virgil,
warding off the flies
that licked the odour of Roman gashes
from the tables of my mind.
I tried for a year
to be useful.

This morning they were a gladiator short.
The keeper of the beasts,
Admetus, a fine, large soldier,
who had such quiet eyes,
green like a tiger's eye through furtive foliage,
had had his arm torn like a leavened crumb
from warm bread
by the Hyrcan tiger
that our commander,
Sextus Posedonius has kept in camp:
a gift from Rome.

By Posidonius's fiat
three slaves, Brigantes youth,
like three ill-fed piglets,
and an ill-fed Roman,
the unloved, unknown me,
will fight presently
with the tiger-men of Roman lust.

West of my villa
everything was incarnadine,
devouring or devoured.

I stand in this pit of stone and sand,
Nemesis,
before your shrine,
(that some foolish artist built
to Roman detriment),
to enjoin upon you my prayer
for vengeance.
I blunt the tip of my sword
in carving my curse
at your feet:
'May Time smack his lips,
like desolate thunder, loud among ruins,
after his gorge of Roman marrow.
And may a desert snarl with dust
and dried spit, now turned into more dust,
like a mad Minotaur, revived from death,
and recollecting the loss of his labyrinth,
in every amphitheatre, even in Rome.'

I will walk out onto the tiger's wrath now
and the Roman cheer.
Let the Hyrcan tiger slit the stone
till its guts lie like sand on the arena.

I can already see myself sinking
in that sand.
It rises around my stormy hair.
It interrupts me,
commands me to be silent in my rage.
It finds me mortal
and willing to part
after every breath.
Unlike Orpheus,
I shall not look back.

Dear Nemesis,
what is the calculus of change required
to find what is lost in the sand,
if what is lost is yourself …?

… There comes the sun,
Nemesis.
The doors are ajar …

(Lullingstone/ Caerleon c. 100 A.D.)

# MARTYRDOM OF ST. ALBAN

It must have been the Autumn.
The leaves had been casting red shadows
in the morning sun. My master
saw them as a benediction. I do not know
what he meant but he seemed
happy, as though he had read
the lines and seen how pink
and free of callous the Christ's palms were.
Imagine. All the ministries that the man
would travel to, all there,
journeys waiting to happen and by reading
them my master almost felt
that he had been chosen to go
with Christ. Their two lives
meeting on a journey. Anyway,
he had gone mad. The late night frost
would only make him take early walks,
and bare-headed. I knew it was
not a good sign. He would stare
at bare boughs on age-wracked trees
as though they were green and eager
spring-sapped ones. He would stare
for hours as though he believed
staring long enough would reverse the seasons.
Mad he certainly was. Romans
are never so bereft of reason.
Even my master was a man of the world
before his head got turned,
like a dromedary in Palestine
before an alien sand-storm,
and north became south. This Jesus
is always south of everything. It is

wrong in a northern land. In
any land, because north is strict.
It is good and honest. The north
helps people live. The south only makes
mad. Believe me, I know. I am
from Galicia. I came with my father
into my master's family. I was an urchin
and Praetor Alban, my master's hoary father
took me in his son-like care. We
rode the stone horse and later ate horse flesh
together. A strong and clever master
he was till this mid-autumn spring
and its poppies in the snow.

&#9733;

The mud sat like a second skin
on that old divine. I asked my master
to have nothing of him. – But out
the divine runs, out of a warren. His nails
would shame the rabbits. He seemed
all summer to have fought the earth.
And yet my master takes him in
like a long lost friend. He clasps
those dirty hands to his bosom,
never minding how hard I work
to keep his coats clean in winter.
He is a shoddy Roman. He
walks all over, you know.
But this! …
And he gave this ermine coat,
one of his best and had the old ferret
dine. – A banquet it was, I tell you. And
at that odd hour of evening. It was snowing.
My master had eaten already.

It was only this sewer priest who ate.
My master sat at his right hand,
with this upstart Christian stroking
his beard like a Sophist
and eyeing the wine with the corner
of his eyes, I am sure. Where had this rat
tasted Roman mead before? I watched
like a child as the candles
made the scene strange and waving,
like a tapestry troubled by the wind
that stood like a ruffian, threatening the peace
at a high window
that I sometimes forget to close.

I saw them sit and talk later.
And my master etched the cross
many times on his breast. I fell
asleep by the third watch. In
the morning I awoke
in an empty house. My master and his bearded fate
had left. On the cold street
my master's name was being shouted
like an emperor's. – I saw him
that afternoon. I was sunk in worry
like a deep pit in the road out of Verulamium.
He called me. I asked him about his shouted name.
He said, the name of the King
of all kings had been shouted louder.
He was truly mad. His new Christian ague
had shaken him badly. He
looked weak, not a Roman. – And then
they said in the square
that my master was killed. The few
pale Christians, they say, are praying.
How I hate them. They say his head

was severed by an axe. Even
a wild Galician like me hates
this Saxon death. But if you tell me
of the Ver going dry and moaning
like a pilgrim to Jerusalem
in a desert where you have to decide
which is more terrible,
to be lost, or losing the hope that you may be found,
as I had heard in one of my master's stories,
I will not believe it. He made up a lot of them.
For me you know. But I never became a Christian.
If you now say that this Ver drying up
like the parched throat after a nightmare,
this last week, the very day my master
was condemned, was this Christian
way of escape, I will say you are not
my friend, but you are a Christian yourself.
Do you not know that the sea drying up
to allow a dusty, old prophet through
is a story I have heard my master tell at a banquet,
many a time,
when I had burned the fish?
No, no and you say the man with the axe
went blind before he struck master down?
What are you? Are you a Saxon?
I knew you to be a gaulic idiot
from Lugdunum. Who tells you
these stories? You tell me that the Saxon chief
did it himself? That he drank last night
till his eyes wept wine? I say,
let the Saxon preserve his mead
and the Roman his wits. All I know
is that my master is gone and I
am no Alban, inheritor
of an old man's words, a young man's blood

and this big, cold house,
like a winter already here
today.

(Verulamium, c. 209 A.D.)

## THE COLCHESTER SPHINX

Many years ago, when I could still jump
like the fishes in shallow summer pools
and run like the deer in the park,
one hot day,
when the tongue of the sky
was white with dust
and thirst,
it rained.

I ran out into the garden
where it smelt only of earth
and yellow grass,
but it seemed the air was waiting
to be a rose;
a rose in the rain,
without essence.

The rain that fell that day was warm,
like the memory of home
hunched with the burden of the sun, —
these raindrops stung my infant cheeks and hair.
I ran shivering in that warm shower.

And there I met him,
at the end of the garden.
It was a strange, green plot
I had never been to.
I did not know how far I had run.
I had outrun my capering days.

I saw him in the rain,
darker than its fall,

half man, half lion:
only the face of a man;
the mane, body and paws
of a lion.

Hewn in a black stone
the face was both old and young.
The rain coursed down his handsome jaw
like black juice from berries,
or grapes.
But he never blinked away the raindrops
and looked at me steadily.

The stone grew soft in my gaze
as rain hit it harder.
I saw my lover in that face.
So much more calm
than all the boys I played with,
my brothers, cousins,
and the sons of other senators and generals.

But why would he not flinch
from my touch or the rain's? —
I had wondered for weeks.
And I was afraid.
As I grew nightly into womanhood,
I was afraid
I would meet him again
at the end of some hot garden,
and that he would refuse
my confused advance
by staring at everything,
as statues do.

On the night of my wedding
I was told
that he was the Sphinx.

I left with my husband
for a northern land,
cold,
in the heat of Capricorn's house
where the sun shivers in furs.

I saw him again,
three days ago.

Through ten years of travel, lovelessness, and politeness,
of kisses from praetors, generals, husband,
visiting senators and other people's children,
I had remained faithful to him.
I had longed to hear
the Sphinx address me,
Virgilia.
I wanted to know who this hero was,
but my husband would not tell me.
I had never read poetry,
or heard the tall bearded men
speak of life.
My brothers did,
but all I learned from them
was swear-words.

Three days ago
I saw him again.

Had he come to pay me a visit?
Was he going to cast the passion
of a girl and a woman in stone,

as he himself was?
Was this a return or a final abandonment?

I saw him at the end of the portico
beside our garden.
It was raining again.
It does a lot here in this country.
But the cold spray had not blighted
the warmth of the autumn afternoon.
It had been almost Roman,
the afternoon,
Rome in late summer.

There was my husband,
sipping wine and pacing the walkway
under the eaves,
and me calling out to him
to come inside for he would catch a cold.

And there was the Sphinx,
sitting,
darker than both day and night,
a face without light or shadow;
a question in stone
when there was no stone to carve.

The lion never twitched its tail
before it pounced.

I knew about lions from the circus.
But I never knew of the lion
who looked at me in the garden
with such fervent unconcern
all those years ago.

Perhaps he haunts all gardens,
far end of all gardens.
I know the Sphinx now.

Outside in the dim afternoon,
workmen draw fire from a stone belly
with chisels.
Another Sphinx is being born.

My husband,
Clodius Pius is dead.

(Camulodunum, c. 300 A.D.)

# THE CUPID OF FISHBOURNE

The chisel hurts my sleep,
rings through my large hands,
shakes my blood
and shapes me through the night,
as I can never shape the marble
lying in the sun.

Seven springs ago,
I was Rufinius, the beautiful,
whom the sky over Mt. Aventinus had promised
ceremonies of light through the days.
I was loved by the maidens
like a god.
Like a god
I loved Vita.
I had pursued her at Ceralia
when I was fourteen and the corn warm
and yellow,
and yielding.
Was I Dis to her Ceres?
I never desired to be away.
I would rather forsake a nether empire.

Things have carved Time,
badly,
like Lucio's satyrs
that gather mold at the far end of the garden.
I feel like the satyrs beneath the Elm.
When the great god made them ugly
they were happy and unashamed;
Lucio, that spitting, shirking truant
made god's ugly, grotesque.

He said, that lout, that he was improving
their looks.
Someone has tried to improve
my time too.

I lie in this season of the stars and the moon
and imagine the Aventine summer.
This is summer too,
they tell me,
but it makes the bone grow hair
to stop the chill.
I lie in the garden often
at this time
as the nights are clearer
and sleep is always half-sleep,
where the less you perceive
the clearer you see. –

Was it hair that went thus?
Like the second coming of the sun, after dark
trying to rescue its mid-day
by making meaningless entrances
on the air,
held taut by a three-day-old moon? –

Rufinius, the sculptor,
the maker of mosaics:
every breath dried by the marble dust,
the breath of rosebushes sets me coughing,
a body that has fallen out with itself
in sheer surprise.
Bony face, scaly skin, slender chest,
and large hands:
a fish, a rock, a branch, a dead root,
I am still twenty-five.

Time has still left me
with the power to count my misfortunes:
the privilege of youth.

I was a free citizen in Rome.
Travel made me a slave.
But can a Roman be a slave,
ever,
even to the will of a fellow Roman? –
Gaius Caelius told me stories of a cold northern land
where I could be the first
to proclaim 'Ars Victa',
well before some peacock general
hoarsely proclaimed 'Roma Victa'. –
The stories had entered my mind
like an unruly wind wreaking havoc
in a house with unbolted windows and doors.

I sailed north:
the last champion of the arts,
the first dunce of the north,
and the south.

This garden reminds me of Aventine slopes:
the Rose, the Lily and the Lavender,
defences against the insurgence of memory.
This is where we work,
Lucio, Porcius and myself.
Others come and go too,
briefly,
too briefly for the remembering of names.
Lucio, the baker, Porcius, the brigand,
who could be safe for society
only in the company of a bit of marble,
and myself,

the legion of 'Ars Victa'
in Noviomagus.

At my villa,
I used to return in the evening,
my mother, Laelia,
sitting on the villa steps, waiting,
to bathe me,
all reeking of musk and the smell
of trodden orchids,
drunken, like the mud.

The trees near my villa
were closer to the sun,
only a thousand miles away.
I shift a rock in this garden
and the roots of a cloud move
over my villa,
a thousand miles away.

I am in my afternoon dream
that has become too prolix
and intruded upon the evening.

I am only a sculptor
and maker of mosaics.
I am given no power over clouds,
only on stone
that is in front of me.

I am old
in my despair,
young in hope.
My land swims away from me,
a furlong each day.

And the unchanging shore,
and seas steadfast to maps
are an illusion that covers this retreat
of lands one desires to be in.

I have made this new mosaic today,
Cupid riding a Dolphin.
Since I will never see Vita again,
(I have not long to live
if the marble and the cold are not kind),
I leave this panel,
plucking the tone-dead Arion
and putting a lovelorn Rufinius
in his stead.
Vita made me sing like a lyre
and I was both Cupid
and Cupid-struck.
I had wings that had a sky in its pits.
The myths changed for many heroes,
would it not change for me today?
Besides, when was the gabbling myth
so privy,
(at secret meetings
the silence of words),
with Vita,
across time?

I have seen miracles before.
The yellow-tuliped slope behind my villa
taking off in fright,
downhill,
chased by winter winds
through the night.
Who needed fireflies or the stars
on such nights

when the owl and the watchers
had their ways illuminated
and fell blind?

I, Rufinius, the sculptor
and maker of mosaics,
have made this garden and this floor
a testament of my return,
if only
to this garden and this floor.

(Noviomagus/Chichester c.308 A.D.)

# WALKING WITH THE ROMANS

You can try on a toga here
without shouldering ice-ages of history,
the squeeze of unthawed estuaries
and the slack of mid-day sleep
against the warm temple of summer
on the Colne. No great citadel
of river and escarpment threatens your stroll.
The paths have been well beaten
by time, in time,
for trudges and loiterings,
tagged and directed by a cartouche
that is all point and no suggestion.

The local council has purged the map
of all malice and mystery.
I thought maps were records of strayings,
not about the dull certainty of finding. –
You could not lose your way in Colchester.
Camulodunum of Claudius:
the site of many a lost Roman trail,
the sojourn of the desperately lost, weather-palled soldiery
that turned into loitering
and moulted into love;
a love deeper than that King Cunobelin
and his brood
held for this wend in the river
when they fled in heaps
the gold, steel and adamant
of the elephants of the imperium.
The angry trumpets of their rage
and the wide, native stare of incomprehension
can still be traced

in some tourist's sounding proboscis
as it disagrees with an unseen fistful of dust
at the museum,
there-about where they let the ashes
of the retired legionaries and their children
die quietly under the halogen.

But then, history, over time,
becomes a pell-mell register of all identity.
The face that frowned, the brow that smiled,
the familiar and the well-loved,
the feared and loathed,
all becoming handy-dandy,
exchanging places,
disfigured despite shouts of no sound.
Loam, sand, rusted iron cacti
of forgotten human ingenuity,
the continuous discontinuity
of aged crag and chiseled stone,
everything, at hand on a Roman walk.

A family from Coimbatore
try on their togas.
The father, looking very soft
and protuberant,
finds his small feet being dragged by large sandals. –
He has found his willing slave,
a British youth, from Wales,
in chains and a metal collar,
(easy and light, the guide assures),
who sidles up to the Roman centurion
from Coimbatore
and tells him in a whisper,
'Take the chain and pull me gently sir'.

Witness Colonia Claudia
this topsy-turvy of time,
the absurdity of all colonies
when forced into time's mad-house. —
Rome triumphs over its Britannia,
Britannia rules the waves,
and did not the rhyme prophecy,
Britons never shall be slaves? —
Here in Colchester's cold autumn,
Coimbatore
leads the Briton in a Roman parody,
shackled, yet smiling.
The owner of the slave smiles too
and gets the slave's autograph
on the back of a Colchester Castle Museum flyer
where his pen slips on the paper
like the rain that trilled down leaves
in another autumn
when Boudicca's name was still under the eaves of time,
and in the sunset after rains
the only burnt figure was the furze.

In Colchester the harrowing of this life
by the one after
is a civic plan.
The route to the after-life
abuts upon Butt Road.
Perhaps it is a well-weathered Roman joke
of a flat-foot walking
over the wakings and slumbers
of Claudius's unquestioning men
and their unquestioning women.

At the museum
a very Roman moment is upon us.
An old tourist is posing bravely
before Boudicca's chariot,
a replica.
Her hand gropes silently for support
till it rests on the chariot wheels;
a nervous snort from the guide,
and her image is on a silver strip,
embossed
for a tenure, not eternity,
smiling before a war-chariot
that forded the blood of thirty thousand citizens.
Now how can that, granted time's prowess
as a harum-scarum interpreter of signs,
be a fond memory,
here or in Japan?
Perhaps it is the incredulity
that makes it Roman.
Were they prepared for this ploughing of time,
up-down, side-to-side?
My autumn haunting shudders
at this stasis of change
in cold Colchester.

(Colchester, City Centre, October 2016)

## WAYSIDE NOTES: PEDDAR'S WAY

No one told me the Romans were here,
or that they had walked
down this cold, earthy trail
leaving this giant footprint
that the map calls a thicket.
A footprint in which mold has been planted
by history,
that scene-of-crime man,
always at hand
whenever nothing happens, –
like an Admetus taking a stroll trying to lighten
a heavy heart
after a light lunch,
or an Agrippina waiting with fallen autumn leaves
for the sun to fall asleep –
trying to plant the evidence of events
that somebody in amnesia's future
might ferret out.

No one told me that there were Romans here,
walking right ahead of me.
I thought I was in Wexford county.

But, not quite.

It seems that I have
a Caius, a Gaius, and a Sextus for company
as they pore over the dog's tail of native routes
and straighten them with the disdain
of a librarian who presses out dog-ears
of what nightly wayfaring scholars are up to,
thus erasing paths.

The sweat and loam underpass here
is built on arches of Roman ribs.
Gaius, Caius and Sextus have engineered
a strong foundation, just lying down,
for eternity,
on their femurs.

The skylark slings its bell and recorder
through some half-buried Roman skull,
bruising the sky with its ricochet.
Tall greenery spreads beneath like the sky's pain.

The hiss of traffic is a proximity
grown strange:
linnets have taken over Peddar's Way.

The soldiers must have felt solitary too.
Finding oneself always is.

No more Romans,
I'll have Wexford please.

## YORK UPENDED

'Looks upside down to me,
but then you're the expert
in these matters.' –
This big man
dressed in the colours of team USA,
hailing from Moldova,
softly spat out the words
padded by his broad, pink tongue.

I did not spot anyone near him,
except a pool of sunshine
that I might have used
as my pot of stagnant tone
and thrown it at a canvas,
if it were mine,
and turned these cold cobbles of York
into a Capri of heat-haze
and rotten olives.

Oddly,
the Romans were there too.
But, those were thawed Romans,
not congealed ones, as here,
in this town of refrigerated autumn
where history has its perennial armory show.

So what's in a Roman column?
Straight-up or upside down
it looks as odd.

At least if it is kicking its heels
into the sky,

it must be Roman and slightly warmer;
more blue perhaps too.

That would be the only roman thing in York though:
roman roots on a roman earth
that has now turned into sky.
The frown of Constantine's architect
grows dark
as only daylight can.

(York, October 2016)

## ACKNOWLEDGEMENTS

Many thanks are due to Todd Stanley Swift, Catherine Myddleton-Evans and Amira Ghanim at Black Spring Press for being so enthusiastic and meticulous in their editing and support.

To Pippa King, thank you for having read my manuscript with such gusto.

My thanks to Wolfgang Goertschacher, Editor of Poetry Salzburg Review, for publishing my poem 'Epistle of Martianus hostilius' in PSR25.